15 REASONS
TO TAKE
GENESIS AS HISTORY

DON BATTEN PH.D.
JONATHAN SARFATI PH.D.

First printing: February 2006
Second printing: August 2006
Third printing: July 2008
Fourth printing: June 2009

ISBN 978-0-94990632-8

Published by *Creation Ministries International*, Brisbane.
P.O. Box 4545, Eight Mile Plains, Qld 4113, Australia.

Visit our website: Creation.com

About the authors

Drs Don Batten and Jonathan Sarfati are scientists with earned doctorates (in biology/plant physiology and chemistry/physics respectively) who have published in secular scientific journals. They work full-time in Christian apologetics as writers, speakers and researchers. Between them they have authored and/or co-authored some of the most widely read books in the world on creation/evolution topics.

CONTENTS

Two millennia ago, the Apostle Paul wrote, 'We demolish arguments and every pretension that sets itself up against the knowledge of God, and we take captive every thought to make it obedient to Christ' (2 Cor. 10:5). In the last 200 years, people have increasingly argued against the knowledge of God, claiming that 'nature is all there is'. They claim that natural processes, alone, can explain the origin and history of everything. This *historical naturalism* sees no evidence for God.

The big bang, uniformitarian geology and biological evolution all *assume* naturalism. Is it then a surprise that all three theories allegedly *support* naturalism?

All three of these ideas contradict the biblical big-picture view of history, which is founded on Genesis 1–11 (not just Gen. 1). However, there are good biblical, historical and scientific reasons to take Genesis 1–11 as a straightforward history of the origin of everything. This booklet presents 15 biblical and historical reasons to take Genesis as history. Other sources cover the scientific arguments.

1. Jesus understood the Old Testament as history

Jesus regarded the OT Scriptures as God's Word; that is, spoken by God or inspired by the Holy Spirit, although written by the hands of men (Matt.19:4, 5; 22:31, 32, 43; Mark 12:26; Luke 20:37) and therefore even the smallest letter or stroke was inspired and would 'never pass away' (Matt. 5:18; Luke 16:17). Jesus cited nearly every book in the OT as authoritative, thus authenticating the canon as we know it.[1] There is no room here for regarding any part of Scripture as deficient in any way due to it suppos-

---

1   Documented in Sarfati, J., The Authority of Scripture, *Apologia* **3**(2):12–16 1994; <creation.com/authority>. Canon: the books that make up the Bible.

edly being the product of the minds of 'illiterate primitives' (campfire stories of Semitic nomads, 'primitive goat-herders', etc.).

A proper hermeneutic (interpretative method) that is consistent with Jesus' attitude involves *exegesis*, or reading *out of* Scripture what the writer was teaching—not *eisegesis*, or reading things *into* Scripture. That is, an honest reading of Scripture entails finding out what God is saying, not trying to make it say what we find acceptable.

This is not 'bibliolatry' (worshipping a book), a term of derision applied to those who accept that Scripture is God-breathed, as it claims. Rather, it is because Christians submit to the lordship of Christ that they take their lead from Him. In many places Jesus said, 'It is written' (in the OT) to settle an argument and, 'Have you not read?' which substantiated the authority of Scripture. Not only was Jesus *not* jealous of the attention men paid to the Bible, He censured them for their ignorance of it (Matt. 22:29; Mark 12:24). In fact, Jesus affirmed the historical accuracy of even the scriptural passages that sceptics most scoff at today.[2] See also Reason 2.

'Inerrancy' derives logically from Jesus' view of inspiration, for how can God inspire error? And if Scripture contains error, then who-

ever decides which parts are in error actually becomes the authority and so usurps God's authority. The ultraliberal 'Jesus Seminar', in which lots are cast to determine which of the words attributed to Christ in the Bible were actually spoken by him, is a logical outcome of such an approach.[3]

Scripture is not authoritative if it is not inerrant: for example, is 'love your enemies' an error, or 'you shall not steal', or 'If we confess our sins, He is faithful and just to forgive us our sins'?

Some say, 'The Bible is authoritative in matters of faith and practice.' This is dangerously deficient: if we cannot trust the Bible in matters of history, for example, how can we trust it in matters of faith and practice (theology)? Luke 16:31 says, 'If they hear not Moses and the prophets, neither will they be persuaded, though one rose from the dead.' And Jesus asked Nicodemus: 'I have spoken to you of earthly things and you do not believe; how then will you believe if I speak of heavenly things?' (John 3:12). So if we can't trust the Bible about earthly things (such as the timeframe of creation and order of events), why should we trust it on heavenly things (e.g. forgiveness of sin, heaven, and moral laws)?

The Chicago Statement on inerrancy is a standard statement among

---

2 Livingston, D., Jesus Christ on the infallibility of Scripture, from 'A Critique of Dewey Beegle's book titled: *Inspiration of Scripture*', MA Thesis, 2003; <creation.com/jesus_bible>.

3 For a critical analysis of this and other faulty Jesus Seminar methodology, see Wright, N.T., *Jesus and the Victory of God*, ch. 2, SPCK, London, 1996.

evangelicals,[4] and concurs with Christ's teachings by affirming 'that what Scripture says, God says. May He be glorified.'

Please note that belief in inerrancy does not mean wooden literalism (a common straw-man argument). We apply the standard, orthodox, grammatical-historical hermeneutic, which recognizes the various forms of writing such as metaphor and hyperbole.[5] In other words, we take as literal history those passages which were clearly intended to be taken as such (including Gen. 1–11). See also our refutations of some other straw-man arguments made by otherwise usually cogent scholars, J.P. Moreland[6] and Wm. Dembski.[7]

2. Jesus regarded Adam, Eve and Noah as historical people

Jesus affirmed many people and events of the past that sceptics deny ever existed or happened: Adam and Eve (Matt. 19:3–6; Mark 10:2–9), Abel (Luke 11:51), Noah and the Flood (Matt. 24:37–39; Luke 17:26–27), Abraham (John 8:56–58), Sodom and Gomorrah (Matt. 10:15; 11:23, 24), Jonah and the great sea creature (Matt. 12:39–41). Either Jesus was mistaken, in which case He does not deserve our worship, or the sceptics and their allies are wrong. Jesus also placed man at the *beginning* of creation, not at the end of billions of years (e.g. Mark 10:6, Luke 11:50–51).[8]

Christ was also fully God, and God never makes mistakes. But some within the church, to justify dismissing Jesus' statements indicating belief in a young creation, assert that Jesus in His humanity was mistaken. This is called the *kenotic heresy*, which abuses Phil. 2:6–11. The 'emptying' was really an *addition* of human nature ('the Word became flesh' John 1:14), *not* any subtraction of the divine attributes. In reality, Jesus voluntarily surrendered the exercise of His powers, e.g. omniscience, independent of the Father's authority (which is why He didn't know the day or the hour of His return), although He could immediately switch them on at will, e.g. to know what people were thinking. But he never surrendered such absolute

---

4 Online at <www.kulikovskyonline.net/hermeneutics/csbe.htm>.

5 A good summary is: Grigg, R., Should Genesis be taken literally? *Creation* 16(1):38–41, 1993; <creation.com/literal>.

6 Ham, K., Wieland, C. and Mortenson, T., Are (biblical) creationists 'cornered'?—a response to Dr J.P. Moreland, *Journal of Creation** 17(3):43–50, 2003; <creation.com/moreland>, *formerly *TJ*

7 Sarfati, J., ID theorist blunders on Bible: Reply to Dr William Dembski, <creation.com/dembski>, 7 February 2005.

8 See also Mortenson, T., But from the beginning of ... the institution of marriage? <creation.com/beginning>, 1 November 2004.

attributes as His perfect goodness, truthfulness, mercy, etc.

Therefore, what Jesus *did* preach, He proclaimed with absolute authority (Matt. 24:35, 28:18). Indeed, Jesus Himself said, 'The words that I speak unto you, they are spirit, and they are life' (John 6:63). He also gave the sober warning:

'If anyone is ashamed of me and my words, the Son of Man will be ashamed of him when he comes in his glory and in the glory of the Father and of the holy angels (Luke 9:26).'

Furthermore, Jesus spoke with the full authority of God the Father (John 5:30, 8:28), who is always omniscient. So if sceptics want to maintain their charge that Christ was mistaken because of His humanity, they must logically charge God the Father with error as well.

These critics also confuse two concepts:

● *Adaptation to human finitude* vs *accommodation to human error*: the former does *not* entail the latter. A mother might tell her four-year-old, 'You grew inside my tummy'—this is simplified rather than false. Conversely, 'The stork brought you' is an outright error. Similarly, God, the author of truth, used some simplified descriptions (e.g. using the earth as a reference frame, as modern scientists do today) and anthropomorphisms, but never error.

● *Limitation vs misunderstanding*: while the Second Person of the Trinity was incarnate in Jesus of Nazareth, He voluntarily limited His omniscience, i.e. in His humanity, He did not know all things. But this does *not* mean that He was mistaken about anything He said. All human understanding is finite, but this doesn't entail that every human understanding is errant.

3. Genesis was written as history

Hebrew uses special grammatical structures for historical narrative and Gen. 1–11 uses those structures. It is the same form as Gen. 12 ff. and most of Exodus, Joshua, Judges, etc. It is not poetry or allegory. Genesis is peppered with the *waw* (*vav*, ו) consecutives (*and...and...and*), which characterize historical writing. The

Hebrew verb forms of Gen. 1 have a particular feature that fits exactly what the Hebrews used for recording history; a series of past events. That is, only the first verb is a *qatal* (perfect), while the verbs that continue the narrative are *wayyiqtols* (imperfects).[9] In Gen. 1, the first verb, *bara'* (create), is *qatal*, while the subsequent verbs

9 Joüon, P. and Muraoka, T., *A Grammar of Biblical Hebrew: Part Three: Syntax*, p. 390, Pontifical Biblical Institute, Rome, 1991.

that move the narrative forward are *wayyiqtols*.[10] Parallelisms, a feature of Hebrew poetry (e.g. many Psalms), are almost absent in Genesis, except when someone is quoted.

The strongest *structural* parallel of Gen. 1 is Numbers 7:10–84. Both are structured accounts, both contain the Hebrew word for day יום (*yôm*) with a numeric—indeed both are numbered *sequences* of days. In Numbers 7, each of the 12 tribes brought an offering on the different days:

• The one who brought his offering on the first day was Nahshon, son of Amminadab of the tribe of Judah. ...
• On the second day, Nethanel, son of Zuar, the leader of Issachar, brought his offering. ...
• On the third day, Eliab, son of Helon, the leader of the people of Zebulun, brought his offering. ...
• On the twelfth day, Ahira, son of Enan, the leader of the people of Naphtali, brought his offering. ...

The parallel is even stronger when we note that Num. 7 not only has each day (יום *yôm*) numbered, but also opens and closes (vs 10 and 84 KJV) with 'in the day that' to refer collectively to all the ordinary days of the sequence. In spite of the use of 'in the day that', no-one doubts that the

numbered day sequence in Num. 7 is anything but ordinary-length days, because these days lack a preposition like 'in'. This refutes the claim by some critics that 'in the day that' (ביום *beyôm*[11]) in Gen. 2:4, summarizing Creation Week, shows that the Gen. 1 days are *not* normal-length. This is a Hebrew idiom for 'when' (see NASB, NIV Gen. 2:4).[12]

In this structured narrative (Num. 7) with a sequence of numbered days, no-one claims that it is merely a poetic framework for teaching something theological and that it is not history. No-one doubts that the days in Num. 7 are ordinary days, so there simply is no grammatical basis for denying the same for the Gen. 1 days. That is, Gen. 1 is straightforward history.

Hebrew scholars concur that Genesis was written as history. For example, the Oxford Hebrew scholar James Barr wrote:

'... probably, so far as I know, there is no professor of Hebrew or Old Testament at any world-class university who does not believe that the writer(s) of Genesis 1–11 intended to convey to their readers the ideas that:

a. creation took place in a series of six days which were the same as the days of 24 hours we now experience

10 See also a statistical analysis of the Hebrew verb forms by Hebraic scholar Stephen Boyd, The biblical Hebrew Creation account: New numbers tell the story, *ICR Impact* **377**, November 2004; <www.icr.org/pdf/imp/imp-377.pdf>.
11 Actually, the verses in Numbers 7 have *bayôm*, where the 'a' represents the definite article, 'the', meaning 'on the day [xth]', unlike *beyôm*, which lacks the article.
12 McCabe, R.V., A defense of literal days in the Creation Week, *Detroit Baptist Seminary Journal* **5**:97–123, Fall 2000; <www.dbts.edu/journals/2000/mccabe.pdf>.

b. the figures contained in the Genesis genealogies provided by simple addition a chronology from the beginning of the world up to later stages in the biblical story

c. Noah's flood was understood to be world-wide and extinguish all human and animal life except for those in the ark.'[13]

Barr, consistent with his neo-orthodox views, does not *believe* Genesis, but he understood what the Hebrew writer clearly taught. Some sceptics criticize the use of the Barr quote, because he does not believe in the historicity of Genesis. That is precisely why we use his statement: he is a *hostile witness*. With no need to try to harmonize Genesis with anything, because

he does not see it as carrying any authority, Barr is free to state the clear intention of the author. This contrasts with some 'evangelical' theologians who try to retain some sense of authority without actually believing it says anything about history.

Other Hebrew scholars who support literal creation days include:

- Dr Andrew Steinmann, Associate Professor of Theology and Hebrew at Concordia University in Illinois.[14]
- Dr Robert McCabe, Professor of Old Testament at Detroit Baptist Theological Seminary in Allen Park, Michigan.[12]
- Dr Ting Wang, lecturer in biblical Hebrew at Stanford University.[15]

4. The rest of the Old Testament takes Genesis as history

A major hermeneutical principle is that Scripture interprets Scripture. We should always consider how other parts of the Bible understand a text.

Exodus 20:11 summarizes the Creation Week. It eliminates any possibility of an extended timescale by *any* interpretive scheme (framework hypothesis, day-age idea, gap theories, God's days, etc.), since it is given as

the basis for our seven-day week with a day of rest (v.10): 'For in six days the LORD made heaven and earth, the sea, and all that is in them, and rested the seventh day. Therefore the LORD blessed the Sabbath day and made it holy.' Note Ex. 20:1: 'And God spoke all these words …' These are the very words of God himself, not the ideas of Moses, or some redactor or even J,

13 Barr, J., Letter to David C.C. Watson, 23 April 1984.
14 Steinmann, A., אחד [echad] as an ordinal number and the meaning of Genesis 1:5, *JETS* **45**(4):577–584, December 2002; <www.galaxie.com/article.php?article_id=5970>.
15 Sarfati, J., Hebrew scholar affirms that Genesis means what it says! Interview with Dr Ting Wang, Lecturer in Biblical Hebrew, *Creation* **27**(4):48–51, 2005; <creation.com/wang>.

E, D or P (long discredited nonsense taught, sadly, at many 'evangelical' theological institutions).[16,17]

First Chronicles 1 summarizes the genealogical data from Adam onwards in Genesis, and many other OT passages affirm the events of Genesis as being historical (real events in time and space).

5. The New Testament takes Genesis 1–11 as history

How does the NT interpret Genesis? There are over 100 quotations from or allusions to Gen. 1–11 in the NT, none of which hint at Genesis being anything but history. Jesus' genealogy (Luke 3) goes back to Adam, 'the son of God,' not the son of an ape! To those who say the early names are mere metaphors we ask: as we trace the lineage back, where do the people stop being real and become metaphors? Hebrews 11 lists heroes of the faith, which start with Abel, Enoch and Noah, without the tiniest hint that they are less historical than the others. 2 Peter 3 refers to creation and the Flood. The Greek verb here is κατακλύζω (katakluzō), a special word referring to the global cataclysm of Genesis; not just an ordinary flood, which is πλημμύρα (plēmmura), cf. Luke 6:48.

The Apostle Paul cites the order of creation of Adam and Eve as well as the fact that Eve was deceived while Adam sinned anyway, and uses this as the basis for teaching on the roles of men and women in the church (1 Tim. 2:13–14). If the first people evolved from a population of apes, then this teaching does not make sense because man would not have preceded woman.[18]

6. Genesis history is consistent with God's nature

Genesis tells us that God spoke things into existence; God speaks and things happen. As it says in Psalm 33:9, 'He spoke, and it was done; He commanded, and it stood fast.'

We should suppose that God Himself would be the best One to tell us what He did, and Genesis, part of God's Word, tells of a rapid creation. This is consistent with other Bible passages about God's authority

16 Grigg, R., Did Moses really write Genesis? *Creation* **20**(4):43–46, 1998; <creation.com/jedp>.
17 Holding, J.P., Does Genesis hold up under critic's scrutiny? (response to critic of ref. 16), <creation.com/moses_critic>, 10 September 2005.
18 See also Sarfati, J., Genesis: Bible authors believed it to be history, *Creation* **28**(2):21–23, March 2006; <creation.com/gen_hist>.
19 Clark, D. *et al.*, Stratigraphic, chronological and behavioural contexts of Pleistocene *Homo sapiens*

being such that He speaks things into existence, *straight away*. Think of the Lord Jesus Christ's dialogue with a faithful centurion in Matt. 8:5–13 as a comparison:

'When Jesus had entered Capernaum, a centurion came to him, asking for help. "Lord," he said, "my servant lies at home paralyzed and in terrible suffering." Jesus said to him, "I will go and heal him." The centurion replied, "Lord, I do not deserve to have you come under my roof. But just say the word, and my servant will be healed. For I myself am a man under authority, with soldiers under me. I tell this one, 'Go,' and he goes; and that one, 'Come,' and he comes. I say to my servant, 'Do this,' and he does it."

'When Jesus heard this, he was astonished and said to those following him, "I tell you the truth, I have not found anyone in Israel with such great faith." … Then Jesus said to the centurion, "Go! It will be done just as you believed it would." And his servant was healed at that very hour.'

As the centurion realized, even his own orders were obeyed immediately and without question. Therefore, he realized, how much more would the commands of the Lord of Creation be obeyed.

In Genesis, we likewise have with the days of creation:

● Command: 'And God said, "Let there be …"'
● Fulfilment: 'And it was so.'
● Assessment: 'God saw that it was good.'
● Closure of the day: 'There was evening, there was morning, Day X.'

That is, God's commands were fulfilled and even assessed within each 24-hour day. Attempts to avoid the clear historical timeframe of Genesis destroy the connection between God's commands and the response of His creation to His commands, making Genesis inconsistent with the rest of Scripture.

7. Genesis as history explains the origin of death and suffering

After God had finished creating everything, he pronounced it 'very good' (Hebrew *tov me'od*). But it is not 'very good' today. Death and suffering now pervade God's creation. But death is 'the last enemy' (1 Cor. 15:26); an interloper.

The Bible clearly teaches that human death came because of the Fall (Rom. 5:12–19 and 1 Cor. 15:21–22). The latter even contrasts the death of the 'first Adam' with the Resurrection from the dead by the 'last Adam', Jesus.

This is a real problem for all long-age views, because according to dating methods accepted by long-agers there are undoubted human fossils 'older' than any possible date for Adam. For example, *Homo sapiens* fossils with evidence of intelligent cultural activity[19,20] have been 'dated' at 160,000 years old.[21] Also, two partial skulls of *Homo sapiens* unearthed in 1967 near the Omo River in south-western Ethiopia have been radiometrically redated to about 195,000 years old.[22,23]

Of course, fossilization requires death. All attempts to marry the Bible with the secular 'natural history' accept the story of *billions* of years. But billions of years of what? These unimaginable eons of time do not float out there on 'cloud nine', disconnected from reality. The fossil record of multicellular organisms supposedly covers some 600 million years in which these creatures were dying and being preserved as fossils. There are fossil bones with cancerous tumours preserved in them; it is a record of suffering and death. In this scenario, man appears about a million years ago, one of the latest results of countless experiments involving death of the unfit and survival of the fittest ('nature red in tooth and claw', as

the poet Tennyson put it). And when man appears, effectively standing on a pile of bones kilometres deep, God says, it's all 'very good' (Gen. 1:31). What an insult to the loving God of the Bible!

How can one make a defence of the goodness of God (theodicy) with *any* of the compromise scenarios that try to retain belief in these millions of years? All one can do is throw one's hands in the air, shrug one's shoulders and give the ground to the sceptics (as so many prominent church leaders have done when questioned over natural disasters). There is only one view of Genesis that provides for a consistent theodicy: when we take it as straightforward history.

Genesis 1 indicates that the animals and people were originally vegetarian (vv. 29–30). We cannot imagine such a world, but it is consistent with visions of a future paradise in Isaiah 11:6–9; 65:25, for example. Animals whimpering in pain and fear while their throats are torn out by others is not consistent with any vision of a future (even partial) restoration, or re-creation, which is always associated with the removal of the Curse

from Middle Awash, Ethiopia, *Nature* **423**(6941):747–752, 12 June 2003.
20 Wieland, C. and Sarfati, J., Ethiopian 'earliest humans' find: a severe blow to the beliefs of Hugh Ross and similar 'progressive creationist' compromise views, <creation.com/ethiopianskull>, 12 June 2003.
21 White, T. *et al.*, Pleistocene *Homo sapiens* from Middle Awash, Ethiopia, *Nature* **423**(6941):742–747, 12 June 2003.
22 McDougall, I., Brown, F.H. & Fleagle, J.G., Stratigraphic placement and age of modern humans from Kibish, Ethiopia, *Nature* **433**(7027):733–736, 17 February 2005.
23 Wieland, C., Redating Leakey's Ethiopian human finds: more problems for compromise, <creation.com/redating>, 18 February 2005.

in Gen. 3, giving rise to an absence of suffering. It is therefore inconceivable to imagine many millions of years of suffering and death as something God would have called 'very good'.

Romans 8:18–25 affirms that the whole creation (not just people) has been 'subjected to futility' and is now 'groaning' and in 'bondage to decay', waiting for its redemption. Leading commentators on Romans such as F.F. Bruce, C.E.B. Cranfield and James Dunn agree that Paul is referring to the Fall.[24] This is consistent with the real history of Gen. 3, where the creation, not just the people, was cursed because of the man's sin. For example, the ground was now to bring forth thorns and thistles (Gen. 3:18). There are thorns preserved in the fossil record, supposedly some 300 million years before man came on the scene. If this is really so, the Bible misleads.

We live in a corrupt creation because of man's sin; God did not create it that way. This has been the view of Christians from the beginning. John Milton's classic poems, *Paradise Lost* and *Paradise Regained*, reflect this Christian worldview that was once accepted almost without question. For example, the great Trinitarian Church Father, **Basil the Great**, Bishop of Caesarea Mazaca, Cappadocia, (AD 330–379) said:

'We see, however, many wild animals which do not eat fruits. What fruit does the panther accept to nourish itself? What fruit can the lion satisfy himself with? Nevertheless, these beings, submitting to the law of nature, were nourished by fruits. ... [But now] the lion is a carnivore, since then also vultures watch for carrion. For the vultures were not yet looking over the earth at the very moment when the animals were born; in fact, nothing of what had received designation or existence had yet died so that the vultures might eat them. Nature had not yet divided, for it was all in its freshness: hunters did not capture, for such was not yet the practice of men; the beasts, for their part, did not yet tear their prey, for they were not carnivores.'[25]

The great Reformer **John Calvin** (1509–1564) agreed:

'Truly the first man would have passed to a better life, had he remained upright; but there would have been no separation of the soul from the body, no corruption, no kind of destruction, and, in short, no violent change.'[26]

'Therefore, we may know, that whatever unwholesome things may be produced, are not natural fruits of the earth, but are corruptions which originate from sin.'[26]

24 For more information, see Sarfati, J., The Fall: a cosmic catastrophe—Hugh Ross's blunders regarding plant death in the Bible, *Journal of Creation* **19**(3):60–64, 2005; <creation.com/plant_death>.
25 Basil the Great, *On the origin of Man* 2:6–7.
26 Calvin, J., *Genesis*, 1554; Banner of Truth, Edinburgh, UK, p. 180, 1984.

The founder of Methodism, **John Wesley** (1701–1791), concurred that the Bible teaches this:

'Why is there *pain* in the world; seeing God is "loving to every man, and his mercy is over all his works?" Because there is sin: Had there been no sin, there would have been no pain. But pain (supposing God to be just) is the necessary effect of sin. [Man] chose evil. Thus "sin entered into the world", and pain of every kind, preparatory to death.'[27]

'But … there were no birds or beasts of prey; none that destroyed or molested another; but all the creatures breathed, in their several kinds, the benevolence of their great Creator.'[28]

David Hull (a non-Christian philosopher of science), wrote:

'Whatever the God implied by evolutionary theory and the data of natural history may be like, He is not the Protestant God of waste not, want not. He is also not a loving God who cares about His productions. He is not even the awful God portrayed in the book of Job. The God of the Galápagos is careless, wasteful, indifferent, almost diabolical. He is certainly not the sort of God to whom anyone would be inclined to pray.'[29]

But according to the Bible, God did *not* create a world like that; it became like that because Adam and Eve sinned. The historicity of the Fall is crucial to an effective theodicy, and this means that hundreds of millions of years of survival of the fittest did not precede Adam and Eve. Note that 'progressive creation' scenarios, while denying evolution, still have hundreds of millions of years of suffering and death as part of God's drawn-out process of arriving at today's world.

8. The Gospel presupposes the historical events of Genesis

Romans 5:12–17, with 1 Cor. 15:20–22; 45–49, grounds the meaning of Jesus' bodily death and Resurrection in the real history of Genesis. A real man, Adam, brought bodily death ('to dust you shall return,' Gen. 3:19) and corruption into God's 'very good' world by his sin. Likewise, a real man, the God-man from heaven, came to undo the work of the first man, the federal head of the human race. As one man brought

---

27 Wesley, J., On the Fall of Man, Sermon 57 (Genesis 3:19), 1872; <http://new.gbgm-umc.org/UMhistory/Wesley/sermons/57>.

28 Wesley, J., God's approbation of his Work, Sermon 56 (Genesis 1:31), 1872; <http://new.gbgm-umc.org/UMhistory/Wesley/sermons/56>.

29 Hull, D., The God of the Galápagos, *Nature* 352:485–486, 1991.

death to all who are in him, one perfect man brings life to all who are in Him.

Furthermore, the historicity of Adam as the ancestor of both the Messiah and of us lies at the heart of the Gospel. Isaiah spoke of the coming Messiah as literally the 'Kinsman-Redeemer', i.e. one who is *related by blood* to those he redeems (Isa. 59:20, which uses the same Hebrew word גואל (*gôēl*) as is used to describe Boaz in relation to Ruth). The Book of Hebrews also explains how Jesus took upon Himself the nature of a man to save mankind, but not angels (Heb. 2:11–18). Jesus can save only Adam's descendants, because only they are related by blood to the Last Adam.

Bishop Hugh Montefiore's *Con-firmation Notebook*, published by SPCK, the Anglican publisher in the UK (1984), shows the baneful consequences to the gospel from denying the Bible's history in Genesis:

'Human beings are the result of evolution, and shaped by natural selection. Self-centredness and aggression were essential at every stage of evolution. Human beings naturally inherit this self-centredness ('original sin') ... What the cross is not ... The Son standing in my place to take the punishment that I ought to have. Such a view is immoral. In any case no one person could suffer the whole world's punishments.'

Such a view is *totally* contrary to the teaching of the NT.

9. A consistent Christian worldview depends on Genesis as history

The Bible tells us of a future where this universe will be purged and there will be a new heavens and earth (2 Pet. 3:10–13). Why? If God created the universe basically as we see it today, which any interpretive scheme designed to harmonize the Bible with the 'deep time' of 'scientific' historical naturalism tacitly accepts, then why would He want to purify it with fire? It does not make sense. However, it makes sense if Gen. 3 is real history (reflected in Rom. 8 etc.). In other words, attempts to accom-modate 'deep time' wreck the Bible's eschatology (i.e. last things, end times teaching).

Furthermore, denial of the historicity of the global Flood also undoes eschatology. Jesus referred to this (Luke 17:26–27). If the account of God's judgment in the Flood is not to be believed, why should we believe the Bible about the judgment to come?

Interestingly, the Apostle Peter prophesied that scoffers would come in the last days, sceptical of Jesus' coming again. These scoffers would say that everything will just carry on as they suppose it has since the beginning. Peter says that they have this philosophy because they are 'wilfully ignorant' of God's revelation that God created things by fiat and that He destroyed the world with a flood (2 Pet. 3:3–6). That's a good description of the naturalistic paradigm that pervades society today, and its effects. Peter also ties the judgment by (global) Flood in with the (global) judg-ment to come by fire (v.7).

Note that the Bible presents Creation and the Flood as being so obvious that anyone who denies their reality is *wilfully ignorant* and worthy of God's judgment (Rom. 1:18–32 and 2 Pet. 3:3–7). If 'evolution' explains our origins such that God's actions are invisible, and there is no evidence for the Flood (modern historical geology), then why does God hold unbelievers culpable?

10. Denying the history of Genesis disconnects Christianity from the 'real world'

People repeatedly say, 'the Bible is not a science textbook', or 'the Bible is about theology, not science', or 'the Bible is about why; science is about how', etc. The late Pope John Paul II advocated 'two non-overlapping magisteria' (religion and science). However, the Bible is largely a book of history, and its theology is rooted in its history. Does it matter whether Jesus actually died and rose again? Perhaps all that's important is what it tells us about loving one another (theological 'liberals' say exactly this). The naturalistic claims of 'science' about the origin and history of the universe are (competing) claims about the very things the Bible tells us and in which it roots salvation: history.

An 'evangelical' theological college in Sydney (Australia) teaches students that Genesis is merely a polem-ic; that it teaches us that God created things and this is a theological statement, not a scientific one. However, 'science' (i.e. the majority view of the current establishment) claims that the universe made itself when nothing exploded in the big bang and that every form of life made itself by purely natural processes from elements created in the big bang; God is not involved or necessary. Either science is making theological claims or the Bible is making scientific claims. It is not possible to solve the problem by word games that artificially segregate knowledge. Such nonsense in the colleges should appal the churches that depend on them for pastoral training.

In 1894, the Scottish theologian, James Denney, wrote:

> 'The separation of the religious and the scientific means in the end the separation of the religious and

the true; and this means that religion dies among true men.'[30]

Quite prophetic; that is exactly what has happened, progressively, since then.

In a survey, children were asked whom they believed, their Sunday school teacher, or their primary school teacher. Eighty percent chose their school teacher. Why? They said that the school teacher taught them facts, whereas the Sunday school teacher only told them stories. Children think this way because that's how many churches teach the Bible: as ethereal stories, disconnected from the real world. Nice stories perhaps, with a moral message, like Aesop's Fables—but not describing things that really happened in space and time.

Likewise, many Christians today have divided their thinking into two compartments: reality and faith; that's perhaps how many Christian academics manage to teach naturalism in their classes and then profess their faith at church on Sunday.

This is called the *fact-value distinction*, which most philosophers reject because no-one has found a clear way of distinguishing between the two. Proponents of this distinction place Christian beliefs in the realm of 'values', i.e. mere personal beliefs that have no connection with reality. Thus, many anti-Christians claim to 'respect' Christianity, but at the frightful cost of dismissing the reality of Christian ideas from any rational discussion.

However, Christianity is a system of *Total Truth* (the title of a book on these issues by Nancy Pearcey). It makes *objective claims* about the world, including its history, and about absolute right and wrong. For example, the bodily Resurrection of Christ is an essential part of the Christian faith (1 Cor. 15:12–19), but it is also a matter of history. It passed the 'testable' claim that the tomb would be empty on the third day, and impinges on science because it demonstrated the power of God over so-called 'natural laws' that dead bodies decay and do not return to life.

Thanks to this 'two compartment' idea, Christianity for many is a blind, existential leap in the dark, taken against reason, or rather aside from reason. It's about having a nice 'worship' experience, or thinking positively, for example. Atheists tolerate such a 'faith', as it makes no truth claims that challenge the unbelief or relativistic ethics of the non-Christian. But this is not *biblical* Christianity. Christian faith is based upon the faithful testimony of those who have seen and heard things *that really happened* (1 John 1:3). It is not a blind, irrational faith. That's why atheists strenuously oppose Christians who defend the truth claims about history in the Bible (Creation, Fall, Flood, Exodus, Resurrection of Jesus, etc.).[31]

30 Denney, J., *Studies in Theology*, Hodder and Stoughton, London, p. 15, 1894.
31 See the introduction and articles re apologetics at <creation.com/apologetics>.

11. The early church leaders accepted the timeframe and global Flood of Genesis

There are two more reasons for analyzing the history of how Genesis has been interpreted:

1. Generally: If long-age interpretations had always been popular, then one could make a case for assuming that the Bible at least hints at this. But if they were absent until they became popular in 'science', it's more likely that such interpretations came from trying to reconcile the Bible with 'science'.

2. Specifically for those who advocate 'deep time' within the church: in order to overcome the charge that they are motivated by 'science' and not the biblical text, they often claim that interpreters throughout history have allowed for long creation days. Therefore it's important to examine the evidence for this claim.

Basil the Great (AD 330–379), in a series of sermons on the six days of creation, the *Hexaëmeron*, argued that the plain meaning was intended—the days were ordinary days; that God's commands instantaneously filled the earth with shrubbery, caused trees to shoot up and suddenly filled the rivers with fish (see Reason 6); that animals did not originally eat each other (see Reason 7); that the sun was created after the earth; etc. He also spoke against evolutionary ideas of humans springing from animals.[32] Note that Darwin did not invent evolution; such ideas go back to antitheistic philosophers before Christ—such as Anaximander, Epimenides and Lucretius. It has been a pagan, anti-God idea from its earliest origins.

Some have misconstrued the church fathers' positions because they have not read them carefully. It was usual in the Eastern Orthodox Church (EO) to view the Creation Week as real, but they often, in parallel, viewed it as typologically pointing to a total Earth history of seven thousand years until the end. They most definitely did not regard the days of Creation Week themselves as long periods.

The late Seraphim Rose, an EO priest, meticulously documented the views of the church fathers of the EO church, showing that they viewed Genesis the way modern creationists do.[33] Dr Terry Mortenson, who

32 Batten, D., Genesis means what it says: Basil (AD 330–379), *Creation* **16**(4):23, September 1994; <creation.com/basil>.
33 Fr. Rose's papers were published posthumously in *Genesis, Creation and Early Man*, Platina, CA, 2000.

earned a Ph.D. in the history of geology, reviewed the book:

> 'His [Rose's] primary sources are early "Fathers" who wrote commentaries on Genesis: **John Chrysostom** (344–407), **Ephraim the Syrian** (306–372), **Basil the Great** (330–379) and **Ambrose of Milan** (339–397). But he also used many other "Fathers" of that and later centuries who wrote on some aspect of Genesis 1–11.'[34]

Rose showed how the EO church fathers were unanimous in their view of the historicity of Creation Week, the Fall and the global Flood. They also believed that God's creative acts were *instantaneous* (see Reason 6). They saw the world before the Fall as profoundly different to that after the Fall.

Some cite **Augustine** and **Origen** to justify the smuggling of 'deep time' into the Bible. These two gentlemen, being of the Alexandrian School, tended to allegorize various passages of Scripture. Their allegorization of the days of creation did not arise from within the text, but from outside influences, namely their adherence to neo-Platonic philosophy (whereby they 'reasoned' that God would not sully himself with being bound by time constraints, etc.). But, contrary to the positions of those who would use Augustine and Origen to prop up their own 'deep time' accommodation, both said that God created everything in an instant, *not* over long periods. And they explicitly argued for the biblical timeframe of thousands of years, as well as the global Flood of Noah.[7]

Some may argue that the church fathers erred in their interpretation, that we now have superior hermeneutical tools. But modern exegetes are not the first who have known about the original languages and cultures of the Bible. The onus is on those proposing a novel interpretation to prove their case.

12. The Reformers understood Genesis as history

Calvin said: 'The day-night cycle was instituted from Day 1, before the sun was created [commenting on "let there be light"]' and 'Here the error of those is manifestly refuted, who maintain that the world was made in a moment [almost certainly referring to Augustine and Origen]. For it is too violent a cavil to contend that Moses distributes the work which God perfected at once into six days, for the mere purpose of conveying instruction. Let us rather conclude that God himself took the space of six days, for the purpose of accommodating his works to the capacity of men' and 'They will not refrain from guffaws when they are informed that but little more than

---

34 Mortenson, T., Orthodoxy and Genesis: What the fathers *really* taught, *Journal of Creation* **16**(3):48–53, December 2002; <creation.com/seraphim>.

five thousand years have passed since the creation of the universe' and 'And the flood was forty days, &c. Moses copiously insists on this fact, in order to show that the whole world was immersed in the waters.'[35]

Luther wrote even more explicitly of these issues, clearly stating his acceptance of the historicity of Genesis. He also dealt with sceptics' claims of supposed contradictions between Genesis 1 and 2.[36]

The opponents of the historicity of Genesis love to refer to historian Ronald Numbers' book, *The Creationists*. Numbers is cited as supposedly showing that young-earth creationism was invented by a Seventh-Day Adventist, George

McCready Price, in the 1920s. This has to be one of the most incredible examples of historical revisionism in existence; on par with the myth (demolished by historian Jeffrey Burton Russell[37]) that the ancients in general, and the church in particular, held to a flat earth. It is as if Numbers, a lapsed SDA, knows nothing of history before Price or Ellen White. The above material on the church fathers and reformers is sufficient to show the error of Numbers' work. But there is much more that refutes it. See the research of the earth science historian Dr Terry Mortenson on the geologists of the early 1800s who defended the biblical age of the earth and the global Flood of Genesis.[38]

13. Atheism requires naturalism—Christians should not deny Genesis as history to accommodate it

The Humanist [atheist] Manifesto specifies belief in the naturalistic origin of the universe and mankind. The latest version (III) specifies 'unguided evolution', but this is a tautology, because evolution is by definition 'unguided' (nature creating nature). Likewise, 'theistic evolution' is an oxymoron (a God-directed undirected process!). And as Reason 7

above points out, the God revealed in the Bible could never have used the senseless bloody process of evolution over millions of years to create a 'very good' world.

The vociferous British antitheist Richard Dawkins said, 'Darwin made it possible to be an intellectually fulfilled atheist,'[39] and many others have said similar things. American athe-

35 Documented in Sarfati, J., 'Calvin said: Genesis means what it says', *Creation* **22**(4):44–45, September 2000; <creation.com/calvin>.
36 Bartz, P., Luther on evolution, *Creation* **6**(3):18–21, February 1984; <creation.com/luther>.
37 Russell, J.B., *Inventing the Flat Earth: Columbus & Modern Historians*, Praeger, 1991.
38 See Dr Mortenson's book *The Great Turning Point*, based on his Ph.D. thesis at Coventry University; <creation.com/turning_point>).
39 Dawkins, R., *The Blind Watchmaker,* p. 6, Penguin reprint, 1991.

ist Will Provine, biology professor at Cornell, made the following point:

> '...belief in modern evolution makes atheists of people. One can have a religious view that is compatible with evolution only if the religious view is indistinguishable from atheism.'[40]

Indeed, evolutionary teaching makes atheists of people. Harvard sociobiologist E.O. Wilson said:

> 'As were many persons from Alabama, I was a born-again Christian. When I was fifteen, I entered the Southern Baptist Church with great fervor and interest in the fundamentalist religion; I left at seventeen when I got to the University of Alabama and heard about evolutionary theory.'[41]

To the atheist, evolution justifies atheism, removing perhaps the best reason that God exists (*creation* demands a *Creator*). So it's not surprising that the most vocal and ardent defenders of evolution and 'deep time' are almost all passionate antitheists.

Evolution (cosmic, geological and biological) claims to explain the origin of everything without reference to any deity. So it contradicts the Bible's teaching that God's attributes are clearly seen from what He has made so that people will be without excuse at judgment (Rom. 1:18–32).

Similarly, God holds scoffers accountable for their *wilful* ignorance of the Flood (2 Pet. 3). All long-age views, which almost by definition accept the uniformitarian interpretation of the geological layers, by the same reasoning reject a global Flood (which would have to have dramatically reworked the surface of the earth).

Evolution is fundamentally a religious idea. Canadian philosopher of science, and anticreationist campaigner, Michael Ruse, said:

> 'Evolution is promoted by its practitioners as more than mere science. Evolution is promulgated as an ideology, a secular religion—a full-fledged alternative to Christianity, with meaning and morality. I am an ardent evolutionist and an ex-Christian, but I must admit that in this one complaint—and Mr [*sic,* actually he has an earned Ph.D. in biochemistry] Gish is but one of many to make it—the literalists are absolutely right. Evolution is a religion. This was true of evolution in the beginning, and it is true of evolution still today.'[42]

Surely, it is the height of foolishness to try to marry the Bible with a religion designed as an explicit substitute for Christianity. We might as well marry it with Baal worship. Ruse later wrote a book claiming that a Darwinian can

40 Provine, Wm.'No free will'; in *Catching up with the Vision,* Ed. Rossiter, M.W., p. S123, Chicago University Press, 1999.

41 Wilson, E.O., *The Humanist,* September/October 1982, p.40.

42 Ruse, M., How evolution became a religion: creationists correct? *National Post,* pp. B1, B3, B7, 13 May 2000; <www.omniology.com/HowEvolutionBecameReligion.html>.

be a Christian, but to him a Christian can deny the Resurrection, which shows how pernicious the Darwinian compromise is.[43]

14. Abandoning Genesis as history leads to heresy and apostasy

Abandoning the historicity of Genesis has repeatedly caused destruction, which we have witnessed first-hand—wrecked individuals, families, churches and nations.

Many prominent, vocal atheists testify to the effect of evolution on causing them to abandon the faith of their parents. The biologist E.O. Wilson, mentioned above, is only one of many. Look at the reasons for the apostasy of Charles Templeton, a former evangelist esteemed by Billy Graham. Templeton raised most of the pseudo-intellectual issues concerning Genesis and historicity[44]—as well as emotional arguments against God's sovereignty, which God has because He is Creator.[45]

A youth minister at an Anglican church in Victoria (Australia) shared with us:

'I used to beat my head against a wall wondering why we lost all our young people at about age 16. In the last few years I've realised that age 16 (year 10) is when they teach evolution in depth in science. Chatting with some of the students I have also discovered that some of the teachers actually identify the Christian students and make a special point of explaining the differences and difficulties in reconciling Genesis and the "facts" of evolution. It's no wonder we lost them. I come near tears just thinking about it.'

Is it any coincidence that church attendance in the western world has declined dramatically since the teaching of evolution in the schools became widespread and systematic (increasingly so since the 1960s in Australia, Britain and America)? Josef Ton, a Romanian Baptist pastor imprisoned for his faith under the communist regime, said: 'I came to the conclusion that there are two factors which destroyed Christianity in Western Europe. One was the theory of evolution, the other, liberal theology ...

43 Weinberger, L., review of *Can a Darwinian be a Christian?* by Michael Ruse (2001), *Journal of Creation* 19(2):42–45, 2005.
44 See Ham, K. and Byers, S., Slippery slide to unbelief: A famous evangelist goes from hope to hopelessness, *Creation* 22(3):8–13, June–August 2000; <creation.com/slide>.
45 Holding, J.P., Review of *Farewell to God*, <www.tektonics.org/books/templefarervw.html>, 9 January 2003.

Liberal theology is just evolution applied to the Bible and our faith.'[46]

A secular source, F. Sherwood Taylor (Curator of the Museum of the History of Science, Oxford) made a similar point:

'... I myself have little doubt that in England it was geology and the theory of evolution that changed us from a Christian to a pagan nation.'[47]

The Uniting Church in Australia is self-destructing following the erosion of scriptural authority beginning in Genesis.

In the US, Princeton Seminary is a classic example: The (otherwise) great Presbyterian theologian Charles Hodge admitted that long ages of Earth history appeared to be at odds with the straightforward Mosaic narrative, but nevertheless, he bowed to the authority of 'science' and so accommodated his understanding of the Bible. Thus, even though he railed against Darwinism as rank atheism, the camel had its nose in the tent. His son and successor, A.A. Hodge, accepted millions of years and toyed with the idea of theistic evolution. His successor, B.B. Warfield (who was conservative enough to sign the well-known 'Fundamentals' document), took this 're-adjustment' of the Scripture to its next logical step, calling himself a Darwinian. The next generation accepted not only Darwinism/millions of years, but questioned biblical authority outright. So conservatives like J. Gresham Machen broke away and founded Westminster Theological Seminary in 1929. As a defender of biblical Christianity, Princeton is no more.

Many 'evangelical' theologians teach that we should reinterpret Genesis because 'science' has 'proven' long ages and evolution. At the same time, they rail against liberal theologians. But the liberals are actually more consistent. They reinterpret the accounts of Jesus' Virginal Conception and Resurrection as unhistorical because 'science' has proven that such miracles are 'impossible'. Although those evangelicals in our Bible colleges who compromise the plain meaning of Genesis have yet to apply their Genesis hermeneutic to the rest of the Bible, there is no good reason not to do so. Compromise with Genesis unlocks the door to doubting the authority of all Scripture, as history has shown repeatedly.

---

46 *New Life* [Australia's weekly Christian newspaper], 15 April 1982.
47 Taylor, F.S., Geology changes the outlook, in *Ideas and Beliefs of the Victorians,* Sylvan Press Ltd, London, p. 195, 1949; one of a series of talks broadcast on BBC radio.

15. Why not take Genesis as history? Only the fallible speculations of historical 'science' stand in the way

Dr Pattle Pun, biology professor at Wheaton College (and a believer in 'deep time'), said what many others, including modern evangelical theologians, have also admitted:

> 'It is apparent that the most straightforward understanding of Genesis, *without regard to all the hermeneutical considerations suggested by science,* is that God created the heaven and earth in six solar days, that man was created on the sixth day, that death and chaos entered the world after the fall of Adam and Eve, and that all the fossils were the result of the catastrophic universal deluge which spared only Noah's family, and the animals therewith.'[48] [*our emphasis*]

So, like Augustine, this approach takes its authority from outside the Bible to reinterpret Genesis to mean something other than its clearly intended meaning. There are many other quotations like Dr Pun's from well-known 'evangelical' biblical and scientific scholars.[49]

In contrast, Dr John MacArthur, noted American evangelical theologian and pastor, remarked:

> 'Scripture, not science, is the ultimate test of all truth. And the further evangelicalism gets from that conviction, the less evangelical and more humanistic it becomes.'[50]

What about science?

This booklet has deliberately not touched on the scientific issues. 'Theology is the queen of sciences.' Indeed, Rodney Stark, for many years Professor of Sociology and of Comparative Religion at the University of Washington, writes:

'I argue not only that there is no inherent conflict between religion and science, but that *Christian theology was essential for the rise of science.* In demonstration of this thesis [I show that] not only did religion not cause the "Dark Ages";

---

48 Pun, P.P.T., *Journal of the American Scientific Affiliation* **39:**14, 1987; Creationists would say that *most*, rather than all, fossils were formed during Noah's Flood, because creationists acknowledge post-Flood catastrophes.
49 Documented in Sarfati, J., *Refuting Compromise,*pp. 55–58, Master Books, 2004.
50 MacArthur, J., *The Battle for the Beginning*, W. Publishing Group, p. 26, 2001.

nothing else did either—the story that after the "fall" of Rome a long dark night of ignorance and superstition settled over Europe is as fictional as the Columbus [flat earth] story. In fact this was an era of profound and rapid technological progress ... the Scientific Revolution of the sixteenth century was the ... result of [Christian scholarship] starting in the eleventh century ... . Why did real science develop in Europe ... and not anywhere else? I find answers to those questions in unique features of Christian theology... .'[51]

This is not surprising, because science presupposes certain axioms, without which it cannot function:

1. The universe is real (because it was created—Gen. 1), not the illusion of Eastern mysticism.
2. The universe is orderly, because God is a God of order not of confusion—1 Cor. 14:33. But if there is no Creator, or if Zeus and his gang were in charge, why should there be any order at all? If some Eastern religions were right that the universe is a great thought, then it could change its mind at any moment.
3. Man can, and should, investigate the world, because God gave us dominion over His creation (Gen.

1:28); creation is not divine.
4. Man can *initiate* thoughts and actions; they are not fully determined by the laws of chemistry. This is a deduction from the biblical teaching that man has both a material and immaterial aspect (e.g. Gen. 35:18, 1 Kings 17:21–22, Matt. 10:28). This immaterial aspect of man means that he is more than matter, so his thoughts are likewise not bound by the makeup of his brain. But if materialism is true, then 'thought' is just an epiphenomenon of the brain, and the results of the laws of chemistry. Thus, *given their own presuppositions*, materialists have not freely arrived at their conclusion, because it was *predetermined by brain chemistry*. But then, why should *their* brain chemistry be trusted over yours or ours, since both obey the same infallible laws of chemistry? So in reality, if materialists are right, then they can't even help what they believe (including their belief in materialism). Yet they often call themselves 'freethinkers', overlooking the glaring irony! Genuine initiation of thought is an insuperable problem for materialism.[52]
5. Man can think rationally and logically, and that logic itself is objective. This is a deduction from the fact that he was created in God's

51 Stark, R., *For the Glory of God: How Monotheism Led to Reformations, Science, Witch-Hunts and the End of Slavery*, p. 123, Princeton University Press, Princeton, 2003.
52 Thompson, B. and Harrub, B., The Origin of Consciousness (two parts article), *Reason & Revelation* **24**(4):25–39, (5):41–55 April & May 2004, <www.apologeticspress.org/articles/498> and <—/496>.

image (Gen. 1:26–27), and from the fact that Jesus, the Second Person of the Trinity, is the *logos.* This ability of mankind to think logically has been impaired *but not eliminated* by the Fall of man into sinful rebellion against his Creator. The Fall means that sometimes the reasoning is flawed, and sometimes the reasoning is valid but from the wrong premises. So it is folly to elevate man's reasoning above that which God has revealed in Scripture.[53] But if evolution were true, then there would be selection only for survival advantage, not necessarily rationality.

6. Results should be reported honestly, because God forbids false witness (Ex. 20:16). But if evolution were true, then why not lie? Unsurprisingly, fraud is an escalating problem in the modern (evolution-dominated) scientific enterprise, as it is in business and politics.

It is no accident that science has flowered since the Reformation, and that this was initially in countries with the strongest concentrations of Bible-centred faith, i.e. Western Europe. And it is no accident that the country today with the strongest remnants of Bible-based Christian faith, the USA, leads the world by a long measure in the output of useful science. And note that when evolution was largely banned in schools during the alleged scientific nadir between the Scopes Trial and *Sputnik,* American schools produced more Nobel prizes than the rest of the world combined. In fact, America produced *twice* as many as all other countries—this was especially pronounced in the biological arena of the Nobels (physiology and medicine), supposedly a field that can't do without evolution.

Thus, it makes perfect sense to begin with what God has said. If we cannot agree that God has indeed spoken, that the Bible is indeed His Word, then we cannot even get started in this discussion. Once we accept that God has spoken and understand what He has said, then we can begin to interpret the 'facts' of history accordingly.

Origins vs operational science

There is a fundamental distinction between the 'science' that deals with history and the science that deals with the operation of today's world. With operational science, you can do repeatable experiments, but you can't with historical science, which deals with past events that are not repeatable. It does not matter much what your religious beliefs are, water still

53 Sarfati, J., Loving God with all your mind: logic and creation, *Journal of Creation* **12**(2):142–151, 1998; <creation.com/logic>.

boils at a given temperature (unless of course you are a postmodernist who thinks that temperature is merely part of the meta-narrative of a Western Christian mindset; a mental construct and only 'true for you'). However, what you believe about spiritual matters profoundly affects what explanations of history and origins you will find acceptable. The late atheist paleontologist Stephen Jay Gould acknowledged this effect of philosophical bias, saying: 'Facts are the world's data. Theories are structures of ideas that explain and interpret facts.'[54]

Biases drive this whole area. The 'facts' of history do not speak for themselves, as most philosophers today realize; they have to be interpreted.[55] It happens to be the case at present that the interpretive framework is pure naturalism. In this paradigm, even 'god' and morals evolved; nothing is 'outside the box'—nature (matter, energy) is all there is. This is shown by the following admission: 'Even if all the data point to an intelligent designer, such an hypothesis is excluded from science because it is not naturalistic.'[56]

James Conant, former president of Harvard University, said about historical 'science':

'The sciences dealing with the past stand before the bar of common sense on a different footing. Therefore, a grotesque account of a period some thousands of years ago is taken seriously though it be built by piling special assumptions on special assumptions, *ad hoc* hypothesis on *ad hoc* hypothesis, and tearing apart the fabric of science whenever it appears convenient. The result is a fantasia which is neither history nor science.'[57]

There is actually nothing in experimental science (the science that has given us so many modern technological benefits) that conflicts with the Bible. It is only the conjectures of historical science ('*ad hoc* hypothesis on *ad hoc* hypothesis') where conflict occurs. As God said to Job, 'Where were you [i.e. were you there] when I laid the foundations of the earth?' (Job 38:4). No paleontologist or geologist was there; they have scraps and bits and pieces in the present, from which they try to construct a story about what happened in the past. But only stories that fit the naturalistic paradigm are permitted.

Whether you believe in revelation or not has a profound effect. Christians believe in revelation: God was there at Creation and no one else was. He has revealed how long He took to do the work and in what order He did it. He also revealed to us that it

54 Gould, S.J., *Hen's Teeth and Horse's Toes,* pp. 254–255, W.W. Norton 1983.
55 Ham, K., 'Where's the proof?' *Creation* **22**(1):39–42, 1999; <creation.com/proof>.
56 Todd, S., Kansas State University immunologist, letter to *Nature* **401**(6752):423, 1999.
57 Cited in Kevin Wirth, Science Education: Only the best *ad-hoc* will do, *Origins Research* **5**(2):2, 1982.

was Paradise; we can only know this by revelation. But the blight of sin spoiled it. Believers look forward to a coming Saviour, the last Adam, who will restore Paradise (Rev. 21–22).

Louis Berkhof, the respected systematic theologian, summed up the priority of Scripture when it comes to these matters:

'Originally God revealed Himself in creation, but through the blight of sin that original revelation was obscured. Moreover, it was entirely insufficient in the condition of things that obtained after the fall. Only God's self-revelation in the Bible can now be considered adequate. It only conveys a knowledge of God that is pure, that is free from error and superstition, and that answers to the spiritual needs of fallen man … Some are inclined to speak of God's general revelation as a second source; but this is hardly correct in view of the fact that nature can come into consideration here only as interpreted in the light of Scripture.'[58]

For much, much more on the problems with compromise with 'scientific' historical naturalism, see the detailed and documented book *Refuting Compromise.*[59]

Why this matters

Those who hold to the historicity of Genesis are often told, 'But it's divisive!' However, according to the Apostle Paul, the divisive ones are those that bring doctrines contrary to Scripture, and Jude included scoffers who deny the global Flood.[60]

Influential atheist philosopher Daniel Dennett described Darwinism in his book *Darwin's Dangerous Idea*[61] as a 'universal acid; it eats through just about every traditional concept and leaves in its wake a revolutionized worldview.' We only have to look at who and what Darwinian ideas have inspired to see the truth of this statement: Marx, Stalin, Mao, Ceausescu, Kim Il-sung, Pol Pot, Hitler, and the eugenics movement (founded by Francis Galton, Darwin's cousin). These offspring of Darwinism murdered over 100 million people and brought untold misery to many more. And we could mention the likes of Australian Peter Singer (now at Princeton University in America where the Hodges and Warfield once taught), who sometimes passes for a 'bioethicist', with his ideas of murdering children and

58 Berkhof, L., *Introductory volume to Systematic Theology,* p. 96.
59 Sarfati, J., *Refuting Compromise,* Master Books, 2004; introductory chapter and several reviews are online at <creation.com/rc-intro>.
60 Batten, D., 'But it's divisive!' *Prayer News—Australia,* October–December 2004; <creation.com/divisive>.
61 Dennett, D., *Darwin's Dangerous Idea: Evolution and the Meanings of Life,* Simon & Schuster, 1995.

the elderly whose lives are deemed to be not worthwhile, while also condoning bestiality. Most atheists hate these connections being pointed out, but they are real.[62]

Of course, this does not prove evolutionary dogma wrong; but if the universe is as the evolutionists claim, then these views and their effects are logical outcomes. 'By their fruit you shall know them.' Jesus was speaking of people, but ideas bear fruit too.[63] Note that our argument is *not* that atheists cannot live 'good' lives, but that there is *no objective basis* for their goodness if we are just rearranged pond scum.[64]

Christians should never compromise with this worldview that brings so much death and misery; a worldview that is an explicit substitute for Christianity, that is anti-Christ and that can destroy their children, friends, or anyone. Christians should obtain their worldview from what the Creator of all has revealed. That is, they should emulate Martin Luther's famous, 'Here I stand' on the authority of God's Word from Gen. 1:1ff; any other authority results in a world running away from its Creator, and in eternally wrecked lives.

---

62 See documentation by European historian Richard Weikart in his book *From Darwin to Hitler: Evolutionary ethics, eugenics, and racism in Germany*, Palgrave Macmillan, New York, USA, 2004; <www.csustan.edu/History/Faculty/Weikart/FromDarwintoHitler.htm>. See also the review, Sarfati, J., The Darwinian roots of the Nazi tree, *Creation* **27**(4):39, 2005; <creation.com/weikart>, and the articles at *Q&A on Communism, Nazism and Eugenics* at <http://creation.com/communism>.

63 Note also, while atrocities may have been committed in the name of Christ, they were *contrary to* Christ's teachings. But atrocities in evolutionary regimes were *consistent with* evolution.

64 Christian philosopher and apologist Dr William Lane Craig explained the Christian moral argument for God in *The Indispensability of Theological Meta-Ethical Foundations for Morality*, <www.leaderu.com/offices/billcraig/docs/meta-eth.html>, 27 September 2003. Sadly, Craig does not accept the teaching of Scripture on the age of the earth, but instead accepts the 'big bang' theory as fact and tries to use it to prove the existence of God.

RECOMMENDED RESOURCES

REFUTING COMPROMISE

The definitive, classic study on the whole subject of 'How do we understand early Genesis?' In his trademark crisp, logical style, scientist and scholar Dr Jonathan Sarfati clinically dismantles those 'positions' on Genesis which do not take it straightforwardly, as history. He also shows how these positions, and their justification (the alleged need to respond to pressure from 'the facts of science'), fail to meet basic standards in the areas of exegesis, logic and the philosophy of science itself.

CREATION MAGAZINE—SUBSCRIPTION

Keep your family informed on the latest easy-to-understand evidences for creation and against evolution. This unique full-colour family magazine gives God the glory, refutes evolution, and gives you the answers to defend your faith. Exciting articles and great witnessing material you won't find anywhere else! Includes a beautifully illustrated full-colour children's section in every issue. Powerful ammunition to intelligently discuss nature, history, science, the Bible, and related subjects. Delivered to your home every three months.

JOURNAL OF CREATION*
—SUBSCRIPTION

You'll enjoy creation science in-depth! A great complement to *Creation* magazine. Read the latest in creation research, stay up-to-date on creation/evolution controversies, and find out the latest flaws in evolutionary arguments. This journal offers analytical and thorough comments in well-referenced articles that will keep you powerfully informed on many topics. A one-year subscription includes three issues, delivered to your home every four months.

*Formerly *TJ*.

FOR MORE INFORMATION ON CREATION/EVOLUTION AND BIBLE-SCIENCE ISSUES, SEE

CREATION.COM

OR CONTACT

AUSTRALIA
Creation Ministries International (Australia)
PO Box 4545
Eight Mile Plains, Qld 4113

Phone: (07) 3340 9888
Fax: (07) 3340 9889
ABN 31 010 120 304

CANADA
Creation Ministries International (Canada)
300 Mill St,
Unit 7, Kitchener, ON N2M 5G8

Phone: (519) 746–7616
Orders & donations: 1-888-251-5360
Fax: (519) 746–7617

NEW ZEALAND
Creation Ministries International (NZ)
PO Box 39005
Howick Manukau 2145

Phone/Fax: (09) 537 4818
A Registered Charitable Trust

SINGAPORE
*Creation Ministries International
(Singapore)*
Clementi Central Post Office
PO Box 195
Singapore 911207

Phone: 9698 4292

SOUTH AFRICA
Creation Ministries International (SA)
PO Box 3349
Durbanville 7551

Phone: (021) 979 0107
Fax: (086) 519 0555

UK & Europe
*Creation Ministries International
(UK/Europe)*
15 Station St,
Whetstone, Leicestershire, LE8 6JS

Phone: 0845-6800-264 (CMI)

USA
Creation Ministries International (USA)
PO Box 350, Powder Springs,
Atlanta GA 30127-0350

Phone: (770) 439-9130
Orders & donations: 1-800-6161-CMI
Fax: (404) 420 2247

OTHER COUNTRIES
Creation Ministries International
PO Box 4545
Eight Mile Plains, Qld 4113
Australia

Phone: +617 3340 9888
Fax: +617 3340 9889